The Surname Hodge

Susan Morris &
Wendy Bosberry-Scott

The question of surnames, their origins, distribution and history, lies at the heart of genealogy as well as being fascinating in its own right.

In the 1980s and 1990s, long before many genealogical sources were even indexed, let alone online, our Surname Report service provided expert assessments of the origins, history and distribution of selected British surnames, using the sources available at the time.

Now, with so many more sources available, we believe that these reports retain their value as studies of individual surnames, and so we are gradually making the Debrett Surname Archive available online and in print for the first time. Some modern indexes have been consulted to refresh and update the reports.

Debrett Ancestry Research Ltd, PO Box 379,
Winchester SO23 9YQ
Tel: 01962 841904
Email: info@debrettancestry.co.uk
Website: www.debrettancestry.co.uk

CONTENTS

Overview

The use of surnames in England began in the Norman period, when surnames were not necessarily hereditary but usually a form of description. Some described the individual's trade or profession; others were nicknames; some gave the father's Christian name; others gave the individual's place of residence or origin.

Different surnames might be used in different documents, or more than one surname given in one document. Early descriptions were fairly elaborate and by the thirteenth and fourteenth centuries these were simpler, but still variable, and indeed the instability of surnames continued until well into the seventeenth century.

Although some Normans would already have had hereditary surnames on their arrival in Britain, the passing on of a surname from generation to generation only became customary in Britain gradually during the course of the thirteenth and fourteenth centuries. At the end of this period most of the population apparently had surnames.

Variations in the spelling of a family's surname continue to be found until the present century. Before this, as most people could not read or write, the parish clerk or other official would write down the name as they heard it.

There are four main groups of surnames:

 A – Local names, which describe a person by his place of residence or origin.

 B – Occupational names, which describe a person by his trade or profession.

 C – Surnames of relationship, which refer to the Christian name of the father or other important relative.

 D – Nicknames or sobriquets, coined to describe a person in terms of his appearance or character.

Many surnames have uncertain origins, but the name Hodge is generally understood to fall into Category C.

Origins

The name Hodge was a medieval pet form of the male baptismal name Roger, which in turn derives from the Old English words *hrothi* meaning 'fame' and *ger* meaning 'spear', the whole name being *Hrothgar* (this is the name of the Danish king in *Beowulf*). The surname Hodge has only one true variant in Hodges, although many other names have been confused with both Roger and Hodge through the centuries.

Two thirteenth century examples of the pet name have been found in Lincolnshire and Cumberland:

1208	Hogge	Lincolnshire Feet of Fines
1212	Hogge	Cumberland Curia Regis Rolls

Chaucer's Cook from *The Canterbury Tales* is named Roger by his host but describes himself by his pet-name 'I highte Hogge of Ware'.

Early examples of the surnames Hodge and Hodges are as follows:

1297	William Hogge	Ministers' Accounts of the Earldom of Cornwall
1327	Alicia Hogges	Somerset Subsidy Rolls
1379	Thomas Hogge	Yorkshire Poll Tax
1379	Ricardus Hoge	Yorkshire Poll Tax
1524	William Hodges	Suffolk Subsidy Rolls

At this point, the surname is represented as Hogge or Hogges and can be found at fairly widespread points of the country. The addition of the final 's', which is frequently found at this period with women's surnames deriving from personal names, is an interesting phenomenon which has never been fully explained, but is often said to be an elliptic form of the genitive: 'Hogge's wife or servant'.

Roger was a common baptismal name and a number of other surnames are derivatives of the pet form Hodge, such as the surname Hodgeman meaning 'servant of Hodge'. Hodgson, Hodgshon, Hodgens, Hodgin, Hodgins, Hodgeon and Hodson are all names that mean 'son of Hodge'. P H Reaney's *Dictionary of English Surnames*, which has been revised by R M Wilson, cites the following diminutives:

> Hodgett, Hodgskin, Hodgetts, Hodgskins, Hodgkin, Hochkin, Hodgkins, Hochkins, Hodgkiss, Hotchkin, Hodgkiess, Hotchkis,
> Hadgkiss, Hotchkiss

However, this work deals primarily with the name Hodge and (in some areas) its variant Hodges.

Hodges is incidentally the surname of one of the editors of the *Oxford Dictionary of Surnames* (1988). Here P Hanks and F Hodges suggest a second source of the surname Hodge as a dialect variation for a nickname deriving from the Old English word *hogg* meaning 'hog' or 'pig'. The Middle English word *Hodge* apparently appears in Cheshire placenames. However, no medieval examples are given that would support this speculation; if the

4

name was used as a nickname we would expect to see 'le Hodge' in the early period.

Distribution

As has been shown, in the medieval period the surname Hodge was found in Cornwall and Yorkshire, while Hodges was found in Somerset and Suffolk, indicating independent origins in several different locations.

In 1890 H B Guppy published his *Homes of Family Names in Great Britain*, still the only published work on surname distribution in Britain as a whole. His work was based on printed genealogies and a survey of county directories for the 1880s, in which he looked especially at the names of farmers, reasoning that they were among the most stable groups in society. He restricted his study to names that appeared in a proportion of 7:10,000 or higher.

Guppy found the surname Hodge principally in Cornwall (24 in 10,000), but also in Devon (16 in 10,000) and Lancashire (11 in 10,000). In Cornwall the name was found especially in the area of Helston and was described as a 'Bodmin name' for a long time, being the names of mayors there at the end of the seventeenth century. In Devon it was particularly common in the Newton Abbott area.

Guppy also noted the variant Hodges in Herefordshire (34 in 10,000); Monmouthshire (33 in 10,000), Dorset (20 in 10,000), Somerset (17 in 10,000), Warwickshire and Kent (15 in 10,000), and Worcestershire (14 in 10,000).

The *English Surname Series* volume dealing with the names of Norfolk and Suffolk has an entry showing that the name Hodges appeared five times in the Norfolk Subsidy Rolls and only once in the Suffolk Subsidy Rolls. This series is as yet very incomplete.

In H R Moulton's *Palaeography, Genealogy and Topography*, primarily a sale catalogue printed in 1930 listing historical documents, ancient charters, leases, court rolls *etc.*, there were six entries for the name Hodge.

31 March 1567
Bargain and sale by John Hodge of Enfield, Middx., to Henry Garlyck (signature), servant to the Queen *[Elizabeth I]* of a house on Enfield Green and lands there.
[sold for £1/15/-]

1 March 1579
Release. St Stephen next. Saltash. Joan Hodge of Trehanne in Saltash, co. Cornwall, widow. To John Paschowe of the same. Witnesses: Willm French of Saltash, Willm Hodge, Willm Pearse.
[sold for 15/-]

5 November 1596
Grant. Enfield. Oliver Hodge als Hogge of Enfield son and heir of John Hodge als Hogge. Henry Hodge als Hogge of London, William Hodge als Hogge of Martyn Abbey co. Surrey. To John Harlow of Enfield. Witnesses: George Kevall, Notary P., Tho Hyll, Alam Noble, Robert Whitbye, Saloman Bulwork (Signatures of grantors. 3 seals)
[sold for 25/-]

24 September 1609

Indenture of lease by Thomas Amirideth, esq., of Brixeham co. Devon, Edward his on, and heir and Lewes Amirideth of the same to John Hodge son of Thomas Hodge, yeoman, of Mollescombe in Stokingham co. Devon, of messuages and land in Stokingham for 3000 years. (Signatures of lessors. 3 seals)

[sold for 25/-]

17 October 1618

Marriage agreement. Edward Wills of Saltash, co. Cornwall. To Edmond Luscombe of Saltash, William Cole of Saltash on marriage of Daniel Dodge to Ifbott daughter of Edward Wills. Witnesses: John Hodge, Oliver Doidge. Signatures: Ed. Luscombe, Will Cole

[sold for £2]

31 August 1641

Indenture of demise by Sir Gregory Norton, Bart., of Densworth co. Sussex to John Hodge, gent. of Moulscombe co. Devon of that part of the said John's messuage in Stokenham co. Devon, being part of the kitchen, and a kilne adjoining, which is built upon the manor lands of Stokenham Prior, for 1000 years. Signature of Sir Gregory Norton

[sold for 20/-]

The surname Hodge was thus found in Surrey, Middlesex, Cornwall and London in the sixteenth century; and in Devon and Cornwall in the seventeenth century. Most names had found their way to the metropolis by this time, but the deeds from Devon and Cornwall confirm Guppy's findings that Hodge is particularly rooted in these two counties: Cornwall was also the home of our earliest example of the surname, William Hogge (1297).

However, the surname is also found many miles away in Scotland. George F Black's authoritative dictionary of *The Surnames of Scotland* lists the following examples:

> Laurence Hoige - witness in Glasgow in 1550 (Abstracts of Protocols of the Town Clerks of Glasgow, Vol 1)
>
> Mariota Hodge - Edinburgh 1625 (Register of Testaments for Edinburgh, 1514-1800, pg. 545)
>
> Thomas Hodge - merchant burgess of Edinburgh 1629 (Charter and Documents of Peebles 1165-1710, pg. 79)
>
> Robert Hodge - born in Scotland, emigrated to America and established firm of Hodge & Shober, Printers

He also has an early example of the form Hodges:

> Thomas Hodgis - burgess of Glasgow in 1487 (Liber Collegii Nostre Domine Registrum Ecclesie, published Glasgow 1846)

Black also quotes a comment from *Surnames of the United Kingdom*, by H Harrison, as follows:

> In England Hodge was so common a rural name that it became a generic term for 'rustic'.

This point, which is supported by several examples in the *Oxford English Dictionary*, is also mentioned under the entry for Roger in Withycombe's *Oxford Dictionary of English Christian Names*, as follows:

> A colloquial use of the name Hodge to denote an agricultural labourer, was an indication of the former frequency of the name.

This colloquial use was still found in the nineteenth century.

Many of the sources available for charting surname distribution through the centuries are necessarily confined to the wealthier sectors of the population: in general, nobody wanted to know the names of the poor but the names of those with money or land were naturally of interest to the authorities. However, one source that covers the whole of the social spectrum is provided by English parish registers, the earliest of which began in 1538 following a mandate that all parish priests should keep a weekly record of all baptisms, marriages and burials that took place in their parish. A survey of a cross section of parish registers for the years 1601 and 1602 was carried out in 1910 by F K and S Hitching; incidences of a particular surname are noted by parish and county, although with no indication of numbers of references.

In 1601 the name Hodge was found in the registers of Bodmin, Constantine and Fowey, all in Cornwall and also in Datchworth in Hertfordshire. Hodges was found in Birchington in Kent and Condover in Shropshire. In 1602, Hodges was noted in the registers of Blisland, St Ervan and St Gluvais in Cornwall, Barnstaple in Devon,

Bocking in Essex and St Botolph in Bishopsgate in London. Hodges was also found in St Botolph, as well as in Condover in Shropshire, Goathurst in Somerset and Broadway in Worcestershire.

A useful guide to the distribution of surnames for the sixteenth, seventeenth and eighteenth centuries in England is provided by the indexes to wills proved, and administrations granted, at the Prerogative Court of (the Archbishop of) Canterbury, in London, which had superior jurisdiction over local ecclesiastical courts where wills were proved until 1858. The PCC thus provides a national index, although it is not a completely representative one, as testators whose wills were proved in the PCC were mostly among the wealthier members of society, and a disproportionate number of them were from London or Middlesex.

A search of the indexes for the years 1584 to 1800 found numerous entries for people bearing the variant Hodges from all over England. Those entries for Hodge wills can be summarised as follows:

1558-1599
Cambridgeshire – 1
Essex – 1
Herefordshire – 1
Hertfordshire – 1
Kent – 1
London – 1
Middlesex – 1
Somerset – 1

Seventeenth Century
Cornwall – 6
Devon – 11

Essex – 1
Kent – 2
Leicestershire – 1
London – 1
Middlesex – 2
Pembrokeshire – 1
Pts – 7
Somerset – 2
Surrey – 2

Eighteenth Century
Cambridgeshire – 1
Cornwall – 10
Cumberland – 1
Devon – 7
Dorset – 2
Hertfordshire – 3
Kent – 37
London – 3
Middlesex – 14
Pts – 19
Suffolk – 1
Sussex – 2
Yorkshire – 1

1800-1857
Argyle – 1
Cornwall – 10
Devon – 14
Dorset – 1
Essex – 1
Gloucestershire – 2
Hampshire – 1
Herefordshire – 1
Hertfordshire – 1
Kent – 5
Lancashire – 1
Lincolnshire – 1

London – 3
Middlesex – 16
Norfolk – 1
Northumberland – 1
Pts – 2
Somerset – 5
Suffolk – 2
Surrey – 2
Sussex – 2
Yorkshire – 2

The PCC was the usual court used for testators who died abroad and in the seventeenth century five Hodge wills were filed for people who had done just that; they died *in partibus* (*Pts*). This number increased in the eighteenth century, but decreased in the nineteenth. In the seventeenth and eighteenth centuries, both Devon and Cornwall have a strong showing of the name, confirming Guppy's description of Hodge as a name well represented in those counties and this follows through into the first half o the nineteenth century. Another nucleus of the name has appeared in the south east of the country, in Surrey, Sussex, Kent, London, Middlesex, Hertfordshire, Essex and Suffolk. It is interesting to see Cumberland appear in the list for the eighteenth century: the personal name Hogge had been noted in Cumberland in 1212. It was relatively unusual for wills from the extreme north of the country to be proved at the PCC as many families would have used the Prerogative Court of York. In fact, several testators from the further reaches of the country appear in the PCC in the first half of the nineteenth century with one testator from Scotland, one from Northumberland and one each from Lancashire, Lincolnshire and Yorkshire.

One interesting will we noted in the seventeenth century listing was for one Alexander Hodge who died in abroad 1690, described as the 'minister of the true Protestant Reformed English Congregation in the city of Amsterdam.'

For the nineteenth century, H B Guppy's survey has been mentioned above. Another important Victorian source is the *Return of Owners of Land of 1873*, sometimes known as the Modern Domesday Book. This source lists, county by county, every owner of an acre of land or more, with their residence (not necessarily the address of their property) and the acreage of their holding.

Return of Owners of Land

Berkshire – Hodges (2)
Cheshire – Hodges (1)
Cornwall – Hodge (17)
Cumberland – Hodge (1); Hodges (2)
Derbyshire – Hodges (2)
Devon – Hodge (14); Hodges (2)
Dorset – Hodges (7)
Essex – Hodges (2)
Gloucestershire – Hodges (12)
Herefordshire – Hodges (12)
Huntingdonshire – Hodge (1)
Kent – Hodge (1); Hodges (13)
Lancashire – Hodges (4)
Leicestershire – Hodges (1)
Monmouthshire – Hodges (13)
Northumberland – Hodge (1)
Oxfordshire – Hodges (2)
Salop – Hodges (3)
Somerset – Hodge (2); Hodges (20)
Southampton – Hodges (1)

Staffordshire – Hodges (1)
Surrey – Hodges (1)
Sussex – Hodges (3)
Warwickshire – Hodges (4)
Wiltshire – Hodges (1)
Worcestershire – Hodges (7)
Yorkshire, East – Hodge (1); Hodges (1)
Montgomery – Hodges (2)

Landowners with the name Hodges owned land in a majority of English counties, stretching in a broad band from the north west of England to the south east even reaching into Wales with an appearance in Montgomeryshire.

Hodge still shows in large numbers in the counties of Cornwall and Devon. It is interesting to see that in Somerset, home of Alicia Hogges in 1327, Hodges is the dominant form, with only two Hodge landowners but twenty named Hodges. There are isolated showings of Hodge in the extreme north, in Cumberland and Northumberland, and also in Kent, Huntingdon and the east riding of Yorkshire.

The first decennial census return in England, Scotland and Wales was taken in 1801, but personal information was only recorded from 1841 onwards. From 1851, the age, occupation and birthplace is given for each member of the household, and so these records provide invaluable genealogical information as well as a fascinating 'snapshot' of the family in the nineteenth century. The latest return currently open to public inspection is that of 1911 and there are now national indexes to the returns from 1841 onwards, although these indexes are not wholly reliable. Using these indexes, we found the following numbers for Hodge in England, Scotland and Wales:

6 June 1841
Hodge (4791); Hodges (5969)

30 March 1851
Hodge (5603); Hodges (6075)

7 April 1861
Hodge (4340); Hodges (5459)

2 April 1871
Hodge (6845); Hodges (7804)

3 April 1881
Hodge (7502); Hodges (8765)

5 April 1891
Hodge (7937); Hodges (8891)

31 March 1901
Hodge (8668); Hodges (10,826)

2 April 1911
Hodge (7591); Hodges (11,774)

As we can see, the numbers for both Hodge and Hodges increase in 1851 but drop back slightly in 1861. Thereafter, Hodges continues to grow and the numbers more than double between 1861 and 1911 but Hodge, after a significant increase in 1871, remains fairly steady increasing by about 500 souls per decade until 1911 when the numbers drop by over a thousand. Some of these discrepancies could be due to the vagaries of the indexes, which are not wholly accurate.

Famous bearers of the name

In Debrett's *People of Today* (1996), the following references to people with the name Hodge were found:

> James William Hodge – Minister for Peking
> Jane Aiken Hodge – author
> Sir Julian Stephen Alfred Hodge Kt. – retired
> Margaret Eve Hodge MBE – MP (Labour)
> Patricia Ann Hodge – actress
> Ralph Noel Hodge – company director

The *Dictionary of National Biography* for the British Isles has the following references to people with the name Hodge and Hodges:

> Arthur Hodge – West Indian planter
> Charles Howard Hodges – painter and engraver
> Edward Hodges – organist and composer
> Edward Richmond Hodges – orientalist
> Nathaniel Hodges MD – doctor
> Sir William Hodges – author
> William Hodges – painter
> Sir William Hodges – chief justice

There are three coats of arms listed in Burke's *General Armory* granted to men of the name Hodge and 13 granted to men of the name Hodges. We list here only those granted to Hodge:

> **Hodge** – (Scotland and Sunderland, co. Durham). Azure a chevron argent between three annulets or. *Crest* – A garb entwined with two serpents proper.

Hodge – Or a chevron gules surmounted by a pale sable. *Crest* – An eagle rising, looking at the sun proper.

Hodge – (impalement Funeral Entry of James Taylour, Sheriff of Dublin, d 20 Dec, 1605, m. Isabel Hodge). Argent three chevronels azure in chief three inescutcheons gules

Printed Genealogies

The following references have been found to printed genealogies that either deal with or mention Hodge and Hodges families:

Hodge
G T Clark, *Genealogy of Morgan and Glamorgan*, 490
Oliver's *History of Antigua*, ii, 75
Miscellaneous Papers Relating to the History, Genealogy, Topography and Antiquity of the British West Indies, iii, 302
C W H Rawlins, *Family Quartette*, (1962), 372
Burke's *Peerage and Baronetage*, (Burkes, 1970)

Hodges
Rudde's *Gloucestershire*, 653
Visitations of Middlesex, 15
Visitations of Somerset, 100, 101
Burke's *History of the Commoners*, 2, 3
Harliean Society, ii, 154: xi, 53
Miscellanea Genealogica et Heraldica, 5th series, V, 247
Reade of Blackwood Hill, 22
Nichols' *History of the County of Leicestershire*, iii, 56
Hutchin's *Dorset*, iv, 460
Baker's *Northamptonshire*, i, 15
Fosbrooke's *History of Gloucestershire*, ii, 44
Burke's *Extinct and Dormant Baronetcies*
Metcalfe's *Visitations of Worcestershire*, (1683), 59
Gloucestershire Notes and Queries, i, 455
Gentleman's Magazine, (1826), i, 291
Visitations of Gloucestershire, 91
Visitations of Somersetshire, 34
Visitations of Middlesex, 19

Oliver's *History of Antigua*, ii, 80

Rev P Whalley, *History and Antiquity of Northamptonshire*, (Oxford, 1711), 2 vols, folio, i, 515

J Burke, *Genealogical and Heraldic Dictionary of the Landed Gentry*, 2nd edition, (1846-48), 2 vols, and 3rd edition, (1860), 1 vol.

Summary

To conclude, the name Hodge derives from a pet-form of the baptismal name Roger. It may well be that other names, such as Hogg, have been confused with Hodge in the past. The form Hodge is less prevalent than Hodges.

Throughout the centuries Hodge has remained numerous in the counties of Devon and Cornwall but is also found in smaller numbers in other areas, notably the home counties and in the extreme north of England in Cumberland and Northumberland.

The variant Hodges can be found throughout the country and has spread to the United States where, in 1969, it was ranked as the 402nd most popular surname in the country (Hodge ranked 573rd). Research in Ireland has found it represented, but not numerous, in the counties of Leinster and Munster.

Sources Consulted

P H Reaney, *The Origins of English Surnames* (London: Routledge & Kegan Paul 1967)

P H Reaney & R M Wilson, *Dictionary of British Surnames* (London: Oxford University Press, 3rd edition 1995)

P H Reaney, *Dictionary of British Surnames* (London: Routledge & Kegan Paul, 2nd edition 1976)

P Hanks & F Hodges, *A Dictionary of Surnames* (Oxford University Press 1988)

M A Lower, *Patronymica Brittanica* (London 1860)

C W Bardsley, *Dictionary of English and Welsh Surnames* (1901: reprinted, Baltimore: Genealogical Publishing Co. 1967)

C L'Estrange Ewen, *Guide to the Origin of British Surnames* (London: John Gifford 1938)

H B Guppy, *Homes of Family Names in Great Britain* (London 1890)

Ernest Weekley, *The Romance of Names* (London: John Murray, 2nd edition 1917)

Ernest Weekley, *Surnames* (London: John Murray 1917)

George F Black, *The Surnames of Scotland* (New York Public Library 1946)

Edward McLysaght, *The Surnames of Ireland* (Dublin: Irish University Press 1977)

T J & Prys Morgan, *Welsh Surnames* (Cardiff: University of Wales Press 1985)

F K & S Hitching, *References to English Surnames in 1601* (Walton on Thames: Bernau 1910)

F K & S Hitching, *References to English Surnames in 1602* (Walton on Thames: Bernau 1911)

Debrett's People of Today (Debrett's Peerage Limited 1996)

The Dictionary of National Biography: Index & Epitome (London 1906)

The Concise Dictionary of National Biography, Part II, 1901-1950, (Oxford 1961)

Burke's Family Index (London: Burke's Peerage Limited 1976)

H R Moulton, *Palaeography, Genealogy & Topography* (1930)

Prerogative Court of Canterbury Wills (online index)

Online index to England, Scotland and Wales census returns 1841-1911

G W Marshall, *The Genealogist's Guide* (1903; reprinted, Baltimore: GPC 1973)

J B Whitmore, *A Genealogical Guide* (London 1953)

Charles Bridge, *An Index to Pedigrees* (London 1867)

Geoffrey B Barrow, *The Genealogist's Guide* (London: Research Publishing Co. 1977)

Sir Bernard Burke, *The General Armory* (London 1884)

C R Humphrey-Smith ed., *Burke's General Armory Volume II,* (Tabard Press 1973)

The Return of Owners of Land (1873)

Eilert Ekwall, *The Oxford Dictionary of English Place Names*

E G Withycombe, *The Oxford Dictionary of English Christian Names* (Oxford: Clarendon Press, 2nd edition 1950)

W J Hardy & W Page, *A Calendar to the Feet of Fines for London and Middlesex: Vol 1 Richard I- Richard III (1189-1485)* (London 1892)

Richard McKinley, *The Surnames of Oxford,* (Leopards Head Press, 1977)

Richard McKinley, *The Surnames of Sussex,* (Leopards Head Press, 1988)

Richard McKinley, *The Surnames of Lancashire,* (Leopards Head Press, 1981)

Richard McKinley, *The Surnames of Norfolk and Suffolk,* (Phillimore 1975)

George Redmonds, *The Surnames of Yorkshire West Riding*, (Phillimore 1973)

Mr Avenell, *The Norman People*, (London 1874)

Debrett's Heraldry, (London 1933)

Boutell's Heraldry (Warne, 1970)

F N Robinson, *The Works of Geoffrey Chaucer* (2nd edition: OUP 1966)

www.ingramcontent.com/pod-product-compliance
Lightning Source LLC
Chambersburg PA
CBHW070245290526
45789CB00004B/1774